Mark Batterson

with Kevin and Sherry Harney

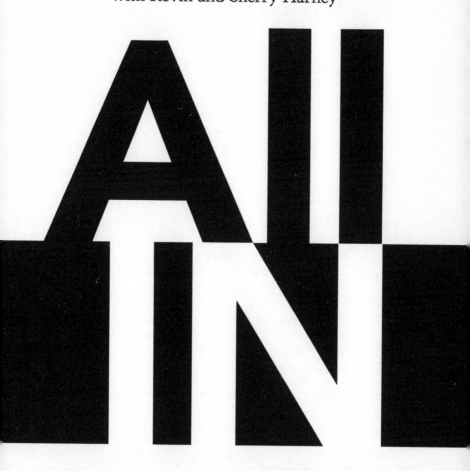

ALL IN

You are one decision away from
a totally different life

ZONDERVAN®

ZONDERVAN

All In Study Guide
Copyright © 2013 by Mark Batterson

This title is also available as a Zondervan ebook.
Visit www.zondervan.com/ebooks.

Requests for information should be addressed to:
Zondervan, *Grand Rapids, Michigan 49530*

ISBN 978-0-310-33313-5

Published in association with the literary agency of Fedd & Company, Inc., Post Office
Box 341973, Austin, TX 78734.

Interior design: Beth Shagene

Printed in the United States of America

13 14 15 16 17 18 19 RRD 21 20 19 18 17 16 15 14 13 12 11 10 9 8 7 6 5 4 3 2 1

CONTENTS

OF NOTE

The quotations interspersed throughout this study guide are excerpts from the book *All In* by Mark Batterson and from the video curriculum of the same name. All other resources — including the small group questions, introductions, and between-sessions materials — have been written by Kevin and Sherry Harney in collaboration with Mark Batterson.

INTRODUCTION

The book *All In* along with this study guide and video are an invitation to experience the kind of life God created you to live. You were designed for more than a life of following a few religious dos and don'ts. Your heart longs for more than an hour of worship each week and a few minutes of devotional reading in the morning.

The Christian faith is not boring, mundane, or safe. It is the greatest adventure any human being can ever experience. It demands all you have and are, and then it demands more.

Over these four sessions you will be challenged to take steps, engage in actions, and follow Jesus in ways you may have never dreamed before. If you are willing to try, God will show up and infuse you with the courage and power you need to begin a new chapter of life and faith.

Below is a manifesto that will give you a picture of where God wants to take you. Read it slowly. Read it carefully. Read it with a heart that is willing to go all in and all out for God!

Quit living as if the purpose of life is to arrive safely at death.
Set God-sized goals. Pursue God-ordained passions. Go after
a dream that is destined to fail without divine intervention.
Keep asking questions. Keep making mistakes.
Keep seeking God.
Stop pointing out problems and become part of the solution.

Stop repeating the past and start creating the future.
Stop playing it safe and start taking risks.
Expand your horizons. Accumulate experiences.
Enjoy the journey.
Find every excuse you can to celebrate everything you can.
Live like today is the first day and last day of your life.
Don't let what's wrong with you keep you from worshiping
what's right with God.
Burn sinful bridges. Blaze new trails.
Don't let fear dictate your decisions.
Take a flying leap of faith.
Quit holding out. Quit holding back.
Push all of your chips to the middle of the table.
It's time to ante up all of your faith.
It's time to go all in.
It's time to go all out.

NOW OR NEVER: PACK YOUR COFFIN

The Christian faith was never meant to be an easy road, a painless journey, or a simple three-step adherence to a set of beliefs. To follow Jesus demands we give everything and invest all we have, and are, for the One who has laid down everything for us. He gave His life for us. The question is: Will we give our lives for Him?

Introduction

He was a pastor, theologian, and author. His book on discipleship, which has since become a classic, was published when he was about thirty years old.

You might wonder: What does a thirty-year-old know about discipleship? What does he understand about the sacrifice involved in following Jesus? Why listen to a relatively young man writing from his ivory tower of the church and surrounded by his theological textbooks?

Before we are too hard on this idealistic preacher, let's hear a bit more of his story. Dietrich Bonhoeffer did not live to celebrate his fortieth birthday. He was arrested by the Gestapo in April 1943 and executed by hanging in a Nazi concentration camp in April 1945. His life ended only three weeks before the Germans surrendered to the Allied Forces and World War II ended.

Why was a German Lutheran pastor imprisoned in a Nazi prison camp for two years and then executed? The answer is simple: because he followed Jesus, no matter what the cost. Dietrich Bonhoeffer was all in. He saw the evil that Adolf Hitler and the Nazi movement was bringing into the world and across his own country of Germany — and he stood in opposition.

He joined a resistance movement because his faith in Jesus and commitment to follow the Savior compelled him to push back. He could not remain idle as countless Jewish men, women, and children were being persecuted and executed. His faith called him to dangerous and costly action.

> "When Christ calls a man, he bids him come and die."
> Dietrich Bonhoeffer,
> *The Cost of Discipleship*

Dietrich Bonhoeffer went all in for the All in All and it cost him everything! In his book on discipleship, aptly titled *The Cost of Discipleship*, he called people to follow Jesus regardless of the consequences. Before he was forty, he had an opportunity to put his writings — based on the teaching of Jesus in the Sermon on the Mount — into practice. As he did, it cost him his life.

Talk About It

What are some ways a Christian can stand up for Jesus in today's society? What are some of the possible consequences we might face if we were to actually stand up in this way?

The complete surrender of your life to the cause of Christ isn't radical. It's normal.

Video Teaching Notes

As you watch the video teaching segment for session one, use the following outline to record thoughts and reflections that stand out to you.

Pack your coffin

Time to go all in

A Copernican revolution ... the inverted gospel

Who's following whom?

Holy dare

God is doing amazing things

What is consecration?

Counting the cost of discipleship

> When you look back on your life, the greatest moments will be the moments when you went all in.

Video Discussion

1. If you packed everything you needed to follow Jesus for the rest of your life into a wooden coffin, what would you take with you?

2. **Read:** Luke 9:23 – 25. When Jesus spoke the words recorded in this passage, He had not yet gone to the cross to die for our sins. What images and ideas must have gone through the minds of Jesus' followers when He invited them to live out the four distinct calls expressed here? In other words, what do you think they thought Jesus was calling them to do when He said:

Deny yourself

Take up your cross

Follow me

Lose your life

How do most Christians interpret and understand these same four callings today?

> We won't come alive, in the truest and fullest sense, until we die to self. And we won't find ourselves until we lose ourselves in the cause of Christ.

3. What are some signs and indicators that Christians in our culture today are playing it safe and not counting the cost of really following Jesus?

When you are operating in "Safe Mode," how does your Christian faith change and begin to look too tame?

4. **Read:** John 3:27 – 30. John the Baptist lived and died with a deep sense of commitment to keep Jesus supreme. His motto, "He must become greater; I must become less," said it all. When you look at the words, ministry, life, and death of John the Baptist, what do you learn from his example of being all in?

5. What are signs and indicators in our daily life that show us — and the people around us — that we have forgotten that Jesus is the center of the universe, not us?

6. Tell about a time in your Christian faith when you were all in, sold out, and unreservedly passionate about Jesus. What led you to that point?

7. Think of the days, weeks, or seasons you are not all in and sold out for Jesus. What leads to such times and what helps you rekindle the fire and get back to a place of full devotion to the Savior?

> *At its core, sinfulness is selfishness. It's enthroning yourself—your desires, your needs, your plans—above all else.*

8. **Read:** Matthew 4:18–22. In this short passage four different men have their own moment of reckoning with Jesus. Each one leaves his nets (his vocation, the family business, his place of security) to follow Jesus. What does this kind of devotion look like today?

What is something you have left (or need to leave) as you follow Jesus with a heart that is all in?

Have you inverted the gospel by inviting Jesus to follow you?

9. Joshua 3:5 says, "Consecrate yourselves, for tomorrow the LORD will do amazing things among you." In the video teaching for this session Mark says, "Consecration means to be set apart. It demands full devotion. It is dethroning yourself and enthroning Jesus. It is the complete divestiture of all self-interest. In short, it is going all in and all out for the All in All." What does consecration look like in your life?

What is one step you need to take in the coming days to consecrate yourself to and for God?

> *Anytime God is about to do something amazing in our lives, He calls us to consecrate ourselves to Him.*

10. Mark shares an honest fear he faces as a pastor. He says, "I'm afraid we've cheapened the gospel by allowing people to buy in without selling out. We've made it too convenient, too comfortable. We've given people just enough Jesus to be bored but not enough to feel the surge of holy adrenaline that courses through your veins when you decide to follow Him no matter what, no matter where, no matter when." Offer some examples of how the church has allowed believers to be too comfortable and how our faith has become too convenient.

What can we do to become more engaged, invested, sold out, and dangerous for Jesus?

Closing Prayer

Take time as a group to pray in any of the following directions:

- Thank God for followers of Jesus who have lived sacrificial and surrendered lives — whether they are people you have met, Bible characters, or people from the history of the church. Give praise to God for their faith, boldness, and example.

- Pray that your life will one day be an example of surrender and passionate commitment to Jesus for those who come after you.

- Thank God for the time you experienced a personal Copernican revolution. If you have not yet experienced this, ask the Holy Spirit to bring you to this place of radical life transformation.

- Tell Jesus that you are ready to deny yourself, take up your cross, lose your life, and follow Him.

> If Jesus is not Lord of all,
> then Jesus is not Lord at all.

BETWEEN SESSIONS

Personal Reflection

Take time in personal reflection to think about the following questions:

- When people look at my life, do they see a person who is sold out and all in for Jesus? If so, what in particular do I think they notice? If not, what needs to change in how I am living my life and following the Savior?

- How are people around me playing it safe, and how might I start taking holy risks for the One who paid the ultimate price for me?

- The early disciples left their nets, the family business, and all the security they had to follow Jesus. What is something I need to leave behind so I can follow Jesus with full devotion?

> You are only one decision away
> from a totally different life!

Personal Actions

Consecration Evaluation

Mark talks about what consecration is not and what it is. He points out that there are many good things that are important, but they are *not* consecration. Here are some examples:

It's not going to church once a week.

It's not daily devotions.

It's not keeping the Ten Commandments.

It's not sharing your faith with friends.

It's not giving God the tithe.

It's not repeating the sinner's prayer.

It's not volunteering for a ministry.

It's not leading a small group.

It's not raising your hands in worship.

It's not going on a mission trip.

Consecration is more than this. It is about complete and utter surrender to God's leading and will. Read the following excerpt from Mark's book and write down three specific things you can do (or not do) that will move you to a place of greater consecration to the Lord.

> The word *consecrate* means to set yourself apart. By definition, consecration demands full devotion. It's dethroning yourself and enthroning Jesus Christ. It's the complete divestiture of all self-interest. It's giving God veto power. It's surrendering all of you to all of Him. It's a simple recognition that every second of time, every ounce of energy, and every penny of money is a gift from God and for God. Consecration is an ever-deepening love for Jesus, a childlike trust in the heavenly Father, and a blind obedience to the Holy Spirit. Consecration is all that and a thousand things more. But for the sake of simplicity, let me give you my personal definition of consecration: Consecration is going all in and all out for the All in All. (*All In*, p. 17)

As I seek to consecrate my life for the work of God in this world, I need to:

1.

2.

3.

Four Things
Jesus was emphatic that those who want to be His disciples will do four things. Set a simple goal that will move you to a deeper place of commitment to do each of these:

1. Deny yourself

2. Take up your cross

3. Follow Jesus

4. Lose your life

Tell a Christian friend about the commitment you have made in each of these areas and ask him or her to pray for you and regularly follow up as you seek to graft these new actions into your lifestyle.

Learning from Those Who Have Gone Before Us

We are all inspired by Christians who have followed Jesus with deep devotion and sacrificial love. During the coming month read one of these books:

Foxe's Book of Martyrs

Prayers of the Martyrs by Duane W. H. Arnold

Bonhoeffer: Pastor, Martyr, Prophet, Spy by Eric Metaxas

Through Gates of Splendor by Elisabeth Elliot

Recommended Reading

As you reflect on what you have learned in this session, read chapters 1 – 3 of the book *All In* by Mark Batterson. In preparation for session two, read chapters 4 – 7.

JOURNAL, REFLECTIONS, AND NOTES

ALL IN: CHARGE!

Many people play it safe, retreat when things get tough, and slip into predictable and familiar patterns. Christians who are all in take risks, charge forward even when it is tough, and are willing to try new things if there is a chance it will forward the cause of Jesus.

Introduction

Jesus knew that the only way to extend grace and forgiveness to broken people was to offer His own life on a cross as a substitution for all of our sins. He committed to do this and nothing in heaven or on earth would stop Him.

When one of His closest friends, Peter, heard Jesus talking about how He was going to willingly suffer and give up His life, Peter tried to stop Him: "Never, Lord!" he said. "This shall never happen to you!" The response of Jesus was shocking and strong. He said to Peter, "Get behind me, Satan! You are a stumbling block to me; you do not have in mind the concerns of God, but merely human concerns" (Matthew 16:22–23).

It was as if Jesus cried out, "Charge!" and pressed forward with no thought of turning back. He could do this because the direction He was heading was in perfect sync with the will of the Father.

Having a tenacious, unyielding, relentless spirit is a glorious gift if you are heading in the right direction and following the leading of God's Holy Spirit, as Jesus was doing. But if you are heading in the wrong direction, it is just sad!

Have you ever watched people charge into situations that were clearly not honoring to God? Such actions can ruin not only their own lives but the lives of those around them. Sometimes it is best *not* to press forward, but to step back, evaluate, and hit the brakes.

> Two thousand years ago, Jesus gave the command to charge! And He's never sounded the retreat!

So, before you yell, "Charge!" the next time, first pause to answer one vital question: Is this the will of God for my life?

If the answer is no, hit the brakes.

If the answer is yes, move forward in confidence.

Talk About It

Tell about a time you felt God call you to take a bold stand or enter into a surprising action for Him. What happened as you pursued this goal?

Faithfulness is not holding the fort. It is an all-out assault on the forces of darkness.

Video Teaching Notes

As you watch the video teaching segment for session two, use the following outline to record thoughts and reflections that stand out to you.

Making a decisive decision to charge!

The inability to do nothing

Jesus, the epitome of passion

Press on

Creating the future

Playing offense

Living in the present tense, not the past tense

Video Discussion

1. Our battles don't look like the ones that Colonel Joshua Chamberlain fought, but we have them nonetheless. Tell about a time you felt outnumbered, shot at, or knocked down. How did you respond in that difficult life situation? How did you experience God's presence with you?

2. Colonel Chamberlain's date with destiny defined his life and future. His decisive action had a much bigger impact than he could have ever imagined in the middle of the battle. What is a battle or challenge you are facing today?

   What is one bold and decisive action you feel God is calling you to take, and what is keeping you from charging forward and taking action?

> *If we do the little things like they are big things,*
> *then God will do big things like they are little things.*
> *That is how the kingdom of God advances.*

3. **Read:** Matthew 21:12 – 13; Matthew 15:1 – 9; and Luke 4:31 – 37. What do you notice and learn about the character, boldness, and strength of Jesus in these accounts?

How do these biblical depictions of Jesus paint a different picture than many of the "tender" and "soft" portraits of Him that are often presented?

4. Mark teaches about how Jesus was never passive but passionate. As you look at Christians today, what are some signs and indicators that we are becoming passive? What are signs and indicators that we are growing more passionate?

How would you describe your heart and lifestyle when it comes to living for Jesus and following Him no matter what the cost? How are you passive and how are you passionate?

5. Respond to this statement: *"Indecision is a decision and inaction is action!"*

What is one decision and action you have been avoiding, and how can your group members pray for you as you seek to charge forward, following God's will in this area of your life?

Take a step of faith in the direction of your dreams.

6. **Read:** Matthew 16:17 – 18. God's people are the church. We are called not to keep the world out, but to attack the very gates of hell and charge forward with the love, truth, and message of Jesus. What are ways you see the church charging forward and making a difference for Jesus in this world?

7. As God's people gathered, the church, we are called to put a full-court press on certain things. What are practical ways your group can press forward and pursue God's will in *one* of the following areas?

- Seeking justice for the oppressed in your community
- Reaching out with the message and grace of Jesus to the lost in your community
- Showing compassion for the hurting and broken in your community
- Strengthening families in your community
- Meeting some other need in your community

The church was never meant to be a noun. It was meant to be a verb, an action verb.

8. **Read**: Philippians 3:12 – 14. Part of charging forward is leaving things behind. What are some of the things Christians need to forget, leave behind, and give up as we press forward toward the high calling of Jesus?

9. What is one thing in your own life that God is presently calling you to leave behind as you charge forward, and how can your group members encourage and cheer you on in this specific area of your life?

God wants to reconcile your past by redeeming it. God is in the recycling business. He wants to recycle the pain, the mistakes, and the suffering and use it for His purposes.

10. We can all be tempted to give up on something that we know God wants us to pursue. His will can be hard, and we can simply wear down and throw in the towel. Checkmark *one* area of your life in which you believe God wants you to charge for-

ward, and then in the space provided write *one* practical step you might take to move ahead.

☐ Your marriage

☐ Your finances

☐ Your health

☐ An addiction you deal with

☐ How you relate to one of your children

☐ A goal you need to set

☐ A kingdom cause you need to enter into

☐ Another area _____

How can your group members pray, support, and encourage you in this area of growth?

Don't sound the retreat. Charge!

Closing Prayer

Take time as a group to pray in any of the following directions:

- Thank God for the people in your life who have followed Him boldly and given you an example of what it means to charge after God, even when it is difficult or scary.

- Pray for eyes to see where you have become complacent and lazy in your faith and lifestyle. Ask God to wake you up, convict you, and move you to fresh action.

- Praise Jesus for counting the cost and taking the cross for you. Thank Him that He never gave up on you.

- Invite the Holy Spirit to help you turn your eyes away from the past and to help you focus on the new things God wants to do in and through you.

> To be fully alive is to be fully present. It mandates leaving the past in the past.

BETWEEN SESSIONS

Personal Reflection

Take time in personal reflection to think about any of the following questions:

- How can I begin my day by asking God to help me take up my cross, deny myself, and follow Jesus? If I do this at the start of each day, how might this shape and direct my choices and actions?

- How do I picture Jesus? Do I see Him as soft and weak, or bold and strong? What can I do to get a more accurate picture of Jesus as powerful, courageous, sometimes confrontational, and always seeking the will of the Father?

- How can I engage in the ministry of my local church in a way that will forward the powerful work of Jesus in our community?

- How can I keep my heart and mind on God's "Plan A" for my life and avoid settling for anything less?

- What ruts do I tend to fall into? How can I identify these and avoid them?

Personal Actions

Offensive Game Plan

Mark tells about how he and his wife take time each year to set a game plan in two specific and important areas of their lives: their calendar and their budget. In each area, they set aggressive goals to serve and honor God. Then as the year goes on, they evaluate and check in on a weekly basis.

If you are married, consider doing this as a couple. If you are single, begin doing this now. If you get married some day, make this a natural part of your lifestyle in that new season of life.

Calendar Goals (Things that will honor God in our/my schedule, such as worship with God's people, personal spiritual growth, serving in the church, serving in the community, time with family, time to invest in friendships, etc.)

Idea:

Idea:

Idea:

Idea:

Idea:

Idea:

Budget Goals (Things that will honor God through our/my use of resources, such as controlling spending, eliminating debt, giving to the church, giving in the community, growing in generosity, etc.)

Idea:

Idea:

Idea:

Idea:

Idea:

Idea:

> *The only way to predict the future is to create it.*
> *You don't let it happen. You make it happen.*

Learning from the Best

The Bible is filled with powerful examples of people who have gone all out for God and charged forward into His will for their lives. During the coming week, study the life of one or two of these great people of faith and learn from their example. Choose from this list:

Noah (Genesis 6 – 9; Hebrews 11:7)
Abraham (Genesis 12 – 18; Hebrews 11:8 – 19)
Joseph (Genesis 37 – 45, 50; Hebrews 11:22)

Joshua (Joshua 1 – 6; Hebrews 11:30)
David (1 Samuel 16 – 21, 26 – 27; 2 Samuel 6 – 7)
Esther (Book of Esther)
Paul (Acts 9, 13 – 28; 2 Corinthians 11 – 12)

Name of the person I chose to study: _____

What I learned from this great person of faith:

Actions I will take because of what I learned from this person's example:

A person I will tell about what I learned and ask to pray for me and keep me accountable as I charge forward in a new area of following God:

Name of the person I chose to study: _____

What I learned from this great person of faith:

Actions I will take because of what I learned from this person's example:

A person I will tell about what I learned and ask to pray for me and keep me accountable as I charge forward in a new area of following God:

Remembering the Past and Pressing Forward

God often called people to set up memorials to remember the great things He had done *for* them and *in* them. These reminders (often a pile of stones) would cause them to look back, remember God's goodness, tell stories of His faithfulness to the next generation, and press on into the future.

List a few ways you can set up memorials to help you and those you love remember God's past presence and power as you press into the future:

God loves when we look back and remember, but He does not want us to dwell in the past. His great works in the past should inspire us to charge boldly into the future. His name is not "I WAS" but "I AM!"

Thank God for the past, but set one or more goals for the future and make a short list of actions you need to take to accomplish these goals in partnership with God. Be sure you don't fall into the old ruts and try to do new things the same old way. You just might need to do new things in a new way. Pray for the Holy Spirit to inspire you with original thoughts, ideas, and ways of following His will for your life.

Going all in is the unwillingness to give up. No matter how many times you get knocked down, you get back up. No matter how tough it gets, you don't give up the fight.

Recommended Reading

As you reflect on what you have learned in this session, reread chapters 4 – 7 of the book *All In* by Mark Batterson. In preparation for session three, read chapters 8 – 9.

JOURNAL, REFLECTIONS, AND NOTES

ALL OUT: RIM HUGGERS

Being all in and living all out for Jesus is about action, taking chances, and following God's will no matter what the cost. It is not enough to simply believe the Bible and have correct information about the Christian faith. We need to do something!

Introduction

Danny was only nine years old, but he loved to fish. All week long he thought about Saturday morning and the fish he would catch. He owned two fishing poles that his uncle had passed down to him back when he was "little." His rods and reels were old and well used, but they worked just fine. He had a tackle box with a broken handle that he had fixed with duct tape. He would get up early every Saturday, pack up his gear, and walk to his favorite fishing spot at the local pier.

On the way, he always walked through the harbor to look at the deep sea fishing boats. He planned to own a boat someday and dreamed of having a business where he would take groups to fish in the open ocean. Each Saturday morning, he would examine the boats and chat with the fishermen.

In the final slip closest to the pier was the most beautiful boat of all — Danny's favorite boat — big and clean, with twin motors, and loaded with deep-sea equipment. The name on the back of the boat, in sharp blue letters, simply read *Gone Fishing*.

Three men owned the boat together, and Danny talked with them for a few minutes every Saturday. They had very nice chairs on the boat and they sat with coffee in hand telling fishing stories to each other and anyone who would stop to talk. "Hey Danny, what do you plan to catch today? What kind of bait or lures will you be using? Do you have any new equipment?"

On many Saturdays they would tell Danny a story or two about fish they had caught back in the good old days. They would point out their new equipment. And they would give him tips about fishing. Danny actually liked hearing their stories but had to pull himself away because he was excited to get out and fish.

> It's time to go all in by going all out.

On his way home, Danny would walk by the *Gone Fishing* crew again, and they would always ask what he caught. And when he would show them his fish, they would invariably tell another story about the days when fish were much larger and more plentiful.

Over time, Danny noticed some things. His three friends with the big boat never left the harbor. Though they had wonderful stories from the past, he realized they did not have any stories about fish they had caught that day, week, or even that year. And though they loved talking about fish, bait, lures, and equipment, it had obviously been a very long time since any of them had actually gone fishing!

One Saturday on his way home from the pier, Danny stopped to show his friends four beautiful fish he had caught. When he left, one of the men sat back in his chair with a smile on his face and shouted, "Danny, if you keep it up, one day you might be a fisherman like us!" The other men grunted in agreement.

Danny looked over his shoulder and with a polite but innocent tone replied, "I *am* a fisherman! You are discussermen!" And he held up his fish as he headed off.

Talk About It

Fishermen go out and catch fish. Discussermen talk about fishing. What does it look like when Christians spend more time talking about faith and less time actually following Jesus? Why is this so dangerous?

There is a world of difference between knowing about God and knowing God.

Video Teaching Notes

As you watch the video teaching segment for session three, use the following outline to record thoughts and reflections that stand out to you.

Rim huggers

Take a hike ... do something

Maximum effort

Picking pomegranates, Saul's complacency

Climb the cliff, Jonathan's courage

Twenty seconds of insane courage

Holy crazy

Going all out for God always starts with the first step of faith. It's often the longest, hardest, and scariest step. But when you make a move that is motivated by God's glory, it moves the heart and hand of God.

Video Discussion

1. Tell about an epic adventure you engaged in and how you experienced what it felt like to "hike the canyon" instead of "hug the rim." How did this experience make you feel alive and connected to God?

2. When Mark was climbing out of the Grand Canyon with his son, exhausted and spent, he saw the people hugging the rim (some of them eating ice cream cones), and this is what ran through his mind: "I felt sorry for *myself*. Then I felt sorry for *them*. I realized that they were *seeing* the Grand Canyon and *missing it* at the same time." Mark says, "You can't truly see what you have not personally experienced." What do you think he means by this statement?

What are some of the dangers when a person stands on the rim and views the Christian faith but never really hikes deep into it and personally experiences what it means to follow Jesus, no matter what the cost?

> *You don't get to know God by looking at Him from a distance. You have to hike into the depths of His mercy and power and love and grace!*

3. **Read:** James 1:22 – 25. James says that when we hear God's Word and understand His will but don't have faith to follow Him, we are deceiving ourselves. Why is inaction and a refusal to be transformed a form of self-deception?

What keeps you from following what you know God wants in certain areas of your life?

4. Mark makes this interesting statement: "Most of us are educated way beyond the level of our obedience. We don't need to know more; we need to do more with what we know." What is he getting at?

What is one area of your life where this is true, and what steps of obedience do you need to take? How can your group members pray for you and help you take steps forward in this area of your life?

> *All it takes is one daring decision! That's all it ever takes.*

5. **Read:** Deuteronomy 6:4 – 9 and Luke 10:27. What does it look like when you love God entirely, completely, and passionately with your:

Heart

Soul

Strength

Mind

Tell about a time you gave God your maximum effort and really invested yourself in loving Him with all you have. What did God do in you and through you as you loved Him passionately?

It's all of you for all of Him.

6. The mission field is on the other side of the world, that's true. But it is also right where you live and work. Take a moment to write down some of the people God has placed in the various mission fields you might serve:

In your home and extended family

At your school or workplace

In your neighborhood

In your social circles

Tell your group members about *one* of these people and how God has moved your heart to love and serve this individual in a way that will reveal the presence and grace of Jesus. How can your group members pray for you and cheer you on in this relationship?

7. **Read**: 1 Samuel 14:1 – 23. What do you learn from Saul's example and from Jonathan's example in this story? How does fear keep us on the sideline of God's adventure, and how does faith move us to the front line of God's will?

8. Tell about an area of your life where fear is keeping you on the sideline. How could a new infusion of faith help move you forward onto the front line of God's will?

How can your group members support you and pray for you as you seek to take a bold step forward and follow God's will for this area of your life?

> Too often we want God to reveal the second step before we take the first step, but if you don't take the first step, God won't reveal the second step!

9. As we follow God's call into difficult and seemingly impossible situations, we encounter "God moments" — times when God shows up and does something we could never have pulled off on our own, so that only He can get the glory. Describe a time you followed God's call (even though it scared you); God showed up; and He got the praise, credit, and glory.

10. Jonathan boldly followed God, propelled forward by the thought, "Perhaps the LORD will act in our behalf" (1 Samuel 14:6). How could your life change if you entered situations and took chances for God, spurred on by that same thought?

The will of God is not an insurance plan. It's a daring plan.

Closing Prayer

Take time as a group to pray in any of the following directions:

- Ask God to make you a canyon hiker and spare you from living as a rim hugger. Pray that you will not miss the adventure of really following Jesus that He has planned for you.

- Invite God to convict and challenge you in areas where you have become a hearer of the Word but need to move into action and become a doer.

- Ask the Holy Spirit to fill you with power and boldness to give a maximum effort as you love God with all your heart, soul, strength, and mind.

- Pray that every day of your life will feel like a mission trip because you are learning to see each person as someone loved by God and in need of the grace of Jesus.

- Invite God to lead and teach you to be holy crazy for His glory and for your good.

> "Eternity won't be long enough to discover all that He is or praise Him for all that He's done."
>
> A. W. Tozer

BETWEEN SESSIONS

Personal Reflection

Take time in personal reflection to think about the following questions:

- Where am I content to be a rim hugger, and what needs to happen so that I can get back into the game, on the front line, living boldly for Jesus?

- What is one biblical truth that I am not obeying? What action do I need to take to be a doer of the Word in this specific area and no longer deceive myself?

- Who is a person I encounter on a regular basis who needs to understand and embrace the love, grace, and call of Jesus? What can I do to introduce him or her to the Savior who has transformed my life?

- What is one cliff I have stopped climbing because my hands were too tired and I became distracted with other endeavors? What can I do to begin climbing again?

- If I believed that God is ready and waiting to act on our behalf, what would I seek to do for His glory?

The phrase all out *literally means: maximum effort.*

Personal Actions

Take a Trip

Mark talks about how valuable and life-changing a mission trip can be. He says that mission trips "turn huggers into hikers!"

If your church plans mission trips, make a commitment to go on one of these and be prayerful and open to whatever God wants to do in you and through you on this trip. If your church does not do mission trips, consider joining a team from another local church and going with them. Or, contact a mission organization such as Compassion International (www.compassion.com), World Vision (www.worldvision.org), or World Mission (www.worldmission.cc) to see if you can join them on one of their mission trips.

During and after your trip, use the journal space below (or a separate notebook) to keep a log of your personal reflections and growth.

*How I would describe the condition of my faith, my passion for God, and my commitment to live out my faith **before** the trip:*

*How I encountered God **during** my mission trip:*

*How God worked **in me** on this trip:*

*How God worked **through me** on this trip:*

What I learned about God's heart for the world:

How God stretched, challenged, and grew me on the trip:

Ways I became a hiker more than a hugger:

*How I would describe the condition of my faith, my passion for God, and my commitment to live out my faith **after** the trip:*

*Ways my life and actions will be different **because of** my mission trip experience:*

When will I go on my next trip?

Twenty-Second Exercise

We all have a short (or long) list of things we feel God wants us to do, but honestly, we are afraid. We don't act because of the possible financial implications, vocational cost, relational challenges, and the list goes on.

Write down three or four things you have a sense God wants you to do, but you have not yet taken action. It could be sharing your faith with a colleague at work, going on a mission trip, beginning to tithe your income, serving at your church, or something else.

Three or four things I really feel God wants me to do:

Example: Serve at my church

1.

2.

3.

4.

What is my fear? (i.e., What is standing in the way of me doing each of these?)

Example: I am nervous there won't be a place of service that really fits who I am and what I can do well.

1.

2.

3.

4.

What action could I take (in twenty seconds or less) to get started and move forward in this area?

Example: I will log onto our church website and investigate possible places I could serve.

1.

2.

3.

4.

> *Your workplace is your mission field.*
> *Your job is your sermon.*
> *Your colleagues are your congregation.*

Learning from Risk Takers

The Bible contains many stories of people who took risks as they followed God. These men and women were not always courageous by nature, but they did hunger to walk with God. In their stories we discover that boldness and courage grow as we learn to follow God's leading, even when we are fearful.

Study one person from this list:

Gideon (Judges 6–7)
Esther (Esther 4–5)
Peter (Matthew 14:22–32)
Mary (Luke 1:26–56)
David (1 Samuel 17)
Elijah (1 Kings 18)
Abigail (1 Samuel 25)

The person I chose to study: _____

What was the challenge and potential fear he or she faced?

How did this person follow God and enter into twenty seconds of insane courage?

What do I learn from this person's example, and how can this help me follow God with greater commitment, passion, and surrender?

> *When did we start believing that Jesus died to keep us safe? He died to make us dangerous!*

Post It and Reflect On It

In the introduction to this study, you read a short manifesto about living each day with an All In spirit. Make a copy of this manifesto (see next page) and post it somewhere you will see it on a regular basis. If you decide to post it publicly, it might just cause someone to ask you what it means. If they do, take a deep breath, and for twenty seconds, tell them you are all in with Jesus and living a life all out for Him!

Recommended Reading

As you reflect on what you have learned in this session, reread chapters 8 and 9 of the book *All In* by Mark Batterson. In preparation for session four, reread chapter 6, and read chapters 10 and 11.

ALL IN MANIFESTO

Quit living as if the purpose of life is to arrive safely at death.

Set God-sized goals. Pursue God-ordained passions.
Go after a dream that is destined to fail
without divine intervention.

Keep asking questions. Keep making mistakes.
Keep seeking God.

Stop pointing out problems and become part of the solution.
Stop repeating the past and start creating the future.
Stop playing it safe and start taking risks.

Expand your horizons. Accumulate experiences.
Enjoy the journey.

Find every excuse you can to celebrate everything you can.
Live like today is the first day and last day of your life.
Don't let what's wrong with you keep you
from worshiping what's right with God.

Burn sinful bridges. Blaze new trails.

Don't let fear dictate your decisions.
Take a flying leap of faith.

Quit holding out. Quit holding back.
Push all of your chips to the middle of the table.
It's time to ante up all of your faith.
It's time to go all in.
It's time to go all out.

JOURNAL, REFLECTIONS, AND NOTES

ALL IN ALL: BURN THE SHIPS

If we are going to go all in and all out for the All in All, it will mean following God's Plan A for our life and not resorting or retreating to our Plan B. In a world where quitting and taking the safe route seems to be hitting epidemic levels, we need to burn the ships, press forward, and quit quitting!

Introduction

Options ... we love them!

Our culture has become enthralled with safety nets, fallback positions, and keeping our options open.

Talk to college students and many will tell you about their dreams, what they really want to do, what they are passionate about. But they will also tell you about how they are hedging their bets and making sure they have a fallback position for their vocational future.

Chat with people who have been in the workforce for a couple of decades and they might tell you about their desire to have a solid retirement and a nest egg to make sure their future is secure. They want to spend their golden years doing some helpful things for others, but they also want to be sure they have enough gold stored up so they don't face any hardships along the way.

You might have even met people who are planning their wedding but are still holding on to their contact list of past romances just in case things don't work out. They are in love and want to be committed to their spouse-to-be, but it seems foolish to burn all their bridges ... just in case.

Some people enter their relationship with Jesus with this same cautious and safety-minded attitude. They like the idea of grace, a friendship with God, the gift of the cross, and the promise of heaven. But if things get tough, they still want a fallback position. They want to keep their options open.

Going all out is all about giving it everything you've got.

During the aggressive persecution of Christians in the first century, many new believers retreated from their faith. Some had been Jewish before meeting the Messiah. Once the heat was turned up, they turned away from Jesus and went back to their Jewish faith. They chose Plan B and missed God's best for their life.

In response to this epidemic of people giving up and giving in, the New Testament book of Hebrews was written to call believers in Jesus to hold on to Plan A, refuse to retreat, and press forward toward God's will. These words found in Hebrews 12:1 – 3 capture the epistle's heartbeat:

> Therefore, since we are surrounded by such a great cloud of witnesses, let us throw off everything that hinders and the sin that so easily entangles. And let us run with perseverance the race marked out for us, fixing our eyes on Jesus, the pioneer and perfecter of faith. For the joy set before him he endured the cross, scorning its shame, and sat down at the right hand of the throne of God. Consider him who endured such opposition from sinners, so that you will not grow weary and lose heart.

Talk About It

How does Hebrews 12:1 – 3 call Christians to a higher level of devotion and commitment, even when times get tough?

It's God's job to get us where He wants us to go. Our job is to make ourselves available anytime, anyplace.

Video Teaching Notes

As you watch the video teaching segment for session four, use the following outline to record thoughts and reflections that stand out to you.

Burn the ships!

Build the ark

Going all out for God

Long obedience

Here I am

Taking one step at a time

Do the right thing for the right reason

*Don't worry about results.
If it's the right thing, then the results
are God's responsibility.
Focus on doing the right thing
for the right reason.*

Video Discussion

1. In a culture that values and encourages leaving our options open, how does a "burn the ships" attitude stand out? Give an example of a time you saw someone burn the ships and slam the door on their options and escape routes.

> Nine times out of ten, failure is resorting to Plan B when Plan A gets too risky, too costly, or too difficult.

2. What would it look like, in very practical terms, to burn the ships in *one* of the following areas of life? Checkmark the area, and then write your strategy in the space provided.

   ☐ Burning the ships back to *past failures*

   ☐ Burning the ships back to *past successes that were part of Plan B*

   ☐ Burning the ships back to a *bad habit*

   ☐ Burning the ships back to *regret*

☐ Burning the ships back to *an unhealthy and ungodly relationship*

☐ Burning the ships back to *crippling guilt*

☐ Burning the ships back to *an addiction*

☐ Burning the ships back to *an old way of life*

> *The first step is always the longest and the hardest. And you can't just take a step forward into the future. You also have to eliminate the possibility of moving backward into the past.*

3. **Read:** Genesis 6 and Hebrews 11:7. Noah and his family built an enormous boat in the middle of a desert, a project that took a hundred and twenty years to complete. Korczak Ziolkowski and his family members have invested more than six decades to carving a likeness of the Native American chief Crazy Horse in the Black Hills of South Dakota — projected finish date 2050! What characteristics and qualities does a person need to press on with a massive and difficult task?

How might a person committed to such a task be viewed by the general population?

> "When your life is over, the world
> will ask you only one question:
> 'Did you do what you were supposed to do?'"
> Korczak Ziolkowski

4. Share a story of someone you know (maybe you!) who has tenaciously pursued a commitment, even when others might have walked away. It could be a spouse who stayed with their husband or wife after a serious accident or the onset of a life-altering illness. Possibly it was an employee who stayed with a struggling company even when there were no raises to be given.

5. The Christian faith demands a devotion to the long haul, long-term commitments, and long obedience in the same direction. What is one way you have learned to increase your commit-

ment, endurance, and stamina as you follow Jesus in the tough times of life?

> If you keep putting one foot in front of the next, it's amazing how far you can go!

6. Mark says this about going all out for God:

It's not a sprint.
It's a marathon.

It doesn't seek fifteen minutes of fame.
It seeks eternal glory.

It doesn't care about public opinion.
It lives for the applause of nail-scarred hands.

It's not satisfied with what the world has to offer.
Its only objective is My Utmost for His Highest.

How does this kind of attitude fly in the face of modern culture with its "pay me now" mindset?

7. If someone followed you with a video camera for a month and recorded everything you said and filmed everything you did, what do you think they would say your life is all about?

If you were to write one short sentence describing why you are on this earth and what you are supposed to do with your life, what would you write?

8. Mark tells his story of pursuing writing because he knew it was something God clearly wanted him to do — even though it took thirteen years for the first signs of accomplishment to become a reality! To follow his calling demanded daily and often painful discipline. What are some ways you need to adjust your lifestyle and priorities to align with what you believe God has placed you on this planet to do?

> *If you are willing to go when God gives you a green light, He will take you to inaccessible places to do impossible things.*

9. **Read:** Judges 3:31, 5:6, and Isaiah 6:1 – 8. Shamgar the judge did not have the right heritage, training, weapon, or support network. But he also did not have any excuses. He took what he had and went out to deliver the people of Israel. Isaiah was trembling in his sandals, but he was willing to follow God. How can being willing to say "Here I am, send me" become the beginning of a whole new adventure of faith?

What is your next step in your journey of following God with passion and commitment? How can your group members pray for you and keep you accountable as you take this step?

> *The litmus test isn't experience or expertise. It's availability and teachability.*

Closing Prayer

Take time as a group to pray in any of the following directions:

- Confess where you have been playing it safe, hedging your bets, keeping your options open. Ask God to help you live all in and all out when you know you are following His will.

- Pray for a patient and enduring spirit as you live for Jesus in the ordinary pursuits of life. Ask God to help you learn to be long-suffering in a world that is quick to bail out and sound the retreat.

- Ask God to give you the power you need to take your next step of faith as you follow Jesus.

- If you have drifted into Plan B, C, or D for your life, ask God to remind you (relentlessly, if necessary), what His Plan A is for your life.

- Thank God for the people you know who have hung in there with tough marriages, walked with kids through long years of struggles, and endured the hard road of life without giving up.

"If a man is called to be a street sweeper, he should sweep streets even as Michelangelo painted, or Beethoven composed music, or Shakespeare wrote poetry. He should sweep streets so well that all the host of heaven will pause to say, 'There lived a great street sweeper who did his job well.'"

Dr. Martin Luther King Jr.

IN THE
COMING DAYS

Personal Reflection

Take time in personal reflection to think about the following questions:

- What ships do I need to burn — and burn right away?

- Where am I about to quit, and how can I hang in there with God's help?

- In what life situation do I need to declare, "Here I am, send me"?

- What is the next step I need to take?

- What might happen if I don't take this step?

> In God's kingdom, calling trumps credentials every time!

Personal Actions

Learning from Hebrews

The book of Hebrews was inspired by God and given to the church at a time when many were leaving or denying their faith because it was dangerous and costly to follow Jesus. They were settling for Plan B when God was offering them Plan A.

Read Hebrews (in one or two sittings, if possible) and answer the following questions:

What do I learn about the goodness of God's Plan A (a life devoted to loving and following Jesus)?

Why is it dangerous to turn back to an old way of life once I have received Jesus and committed to follow Him?

How is Jesus better than the ancient ways of faith that many of the people still wanted to cling to?

How does holding to Jesus and following Him — even in the hard times — bring the greatest joy, hope, and life?

Sharpening Your Tool

If we can use any tool to bring glory to God, it makes sense to develop our skills and sharpen our tools so that we can bring Him the maximum glory. What is one tool God has called you to use?

What are three ways you can sharpen and strengthen this tool?

1.

2.

3.

During the coming weeks, intentionally and actively work at sharpening this tool of your trade. Pray that God will help you use it to the best of your ability and for His glory.

> No matter what tool you use in your trade—
> a hammer, a keyboard, a mop, a football,
> a spreadsheet, a microphone, an MRI,
> or an espresso machine—it's an act of obedience.
> It's the mechanism whereby you worship God.

No More Excuses

Study the excuses of Gideon and Moses (Judges 6:11 – 18; Exodus 3:4 – 14). Then, choose *one* of the men and write down each excuse he made when God called him to follow Him and take action:

Excuse # _____

Excuse # _____

Excuse # _____

Excuse # _____

Excuse # _____

Excuse # _____

How do I see myself make similar excuses when God calls me to follow Him and take chances for His glory? What can I do to abandon these excuses and say, "Here I am, send me"?

God doesn't call the qualified.
He qualifies the called.

Recommended Reading

As you reflect on what you have learned in this session, reread chapters 6, 10, and 11 of the book *All In* by Mark Batterson. Read chapters 12 – 17 as well.

JOURNAL, REFLECTIONS, AND NOTES

SMALL GROUP LEADER HELPS

To ensure a successful small group experience, read the following information before beginning.

Group Preparation

Whether your small group has been meeting together for years or is gathering for the first time, be sure to designate a consistent time and place to work through the four sessions. Once you establish the when and where of your times together, select a facilitator who will keep discussions on track and an eye on the clock. If you choose to rotate this responsibility, assign the four sessions to their respective facilitators up front, so that group members can prepare their thoughts and questions prior to the session they are responsible for leading. Follow the same assignment procedure should your group want to serve any snacks or beverages.

A Note to Facilitators

As facilitator, you are responsible for honoring the agreed-upon time frame of each meeting, for prompting helpful discussion among your group, and for keeping the dialogue equitable by drawing out quieter members and helping more talkative members to remember that others' insights are valued in your group.

You might find it helpful to preview each session's video teaching segment and then scan the "Video Discussion" questions that pertain to it, highlighting various questions that you want to be sure to cover during your group's meeting. Ask God in advance of your time together to guide your group's discussion, and then be sensitive to the direction He wishes to lead.

Urge participants to bring their study guide, pen, and a Bible to every gathering. Encourage them to consider buying a copy of the *All In* book by Mark Batterson to supplement this study.

Session Format

Each session of the study guide includes the following group components:

- **"Introduction"** — an entrée to the session's topic, which may be read by a volunteer or summarized by the facilitator

- **"Talk About It"** — an icebreaker question that relates to the session topic and invites input from every group member

- **"Video Teaching Notes"** — an outline of the session's video teaching (about 18 minutes each) for group members to follow along and take notes if they wish

- **"Video Discussion"** — video-related and Bible exploration questions that reinforce the session content and elicit personal input from every group member

- **"Closing Prayer"** — several prayer cues to guide group members in closing prayer

Additionally, in each session you will find a **"Between Sessions"** section (for session four, **"In the Coming Days"**) that includes suggestions for personal response, recommended reading from the *All In* book, and journal pages.

All In

You Are One Decision Away from a Totally Different Life

Mark Batterson, New York Times *bestselling author*

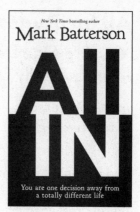

Half way is no way to live! Quit holding back. Quit holding out. It's time to go all in and all out for God.

If Jesus hung on His cross for us, the least we can do is carry our cross for Him. And the good news is this: If you don't hold out on God, God won't hold out on you. In reality, no one has ever truly sacrificed anything for God because the eternal reward always outweighs the temporal discomfort.

Many people believe they are following Jesus, but they have mistakenly invited Jesus to follow them. Mark Batterson calls it "the inverted gospel." In *All In*, he challenges you to fully surrender your life to the lordship of Jesus Christ. That is when the true adventure begins.

All In: Student Edition

You Are One Decision Away From a Totally Different Life

Mark Batterson
with Parker Batterson

The gospel costs nothing — it's a free gift, compliments of God's grace. But while it doesn't cost anything, it demands everything — including that we go "all in," a term that means placing all that you own into the game of life. And that's where many of us get stuck. What if we miss out on what this life has to offer?

The truth is, the only thing you'll miss out on is everything God has to offer. Inside these pages, Mark Batterson shares vivid stories of people going all in for a greater purpose, ranging from the against-all-odds defense of Little Round Top in the Civil War to the lives of biblical characters like Shamgar and Moses and Elijah and Caleb and … Judas.

The message of *All In Student Edition* is simple: if Jesus is not Lord of all, then Jesus is not Lord at all. It's all or nothing. It's now or never. Jesus gave all of Himself for you on Calvary's cross. He wants all of you in return. In essence, your life is not your own — but it can be more amazing than you ever dared imagine if you decide to go all in.

Available in stores and online!

The Circle Maker Curriculum Kit

Praying Circles Around Your Biggest Dreams and Greatest Fears

Mark Batterson

This dynamic four-week church campaign uses the story of Honi the circle maker, who prayer-walked his way around a devastating drought in first-century BC Israel until the rains came, to help you and your entire church begin to identify the dreams and future miracles to draw circles around to find your answers from God.

Four video sessions expand on the teaching from Mark Batterson's book of the same name and combine a teaching element with a creative element to draw you into the circle. The participant's guide provides teaching notes, discussion questions, Bible study, and between-session activities. Each session wraps up with a practical application called "Draw the Circle," giving you the opportunity to put the prayer principles you have learned into practice.

This curriculum kit includes:

- one hardcover book
- one participant's guide
- one DVD-ROM containing four small-group video sessions, a getting started guide, four sermon outlines, and all the church promotional materials needed to successfully launch and sustain a four-week church experience.
- one "Getting Started" guide

The curriculum can be used in a variety of ways — as a whole church campaign (adult congregation), adult Sunday school, small-group study, or individual use.

Available in stores and online!

Share Your Thoughts

With the Author: Your comments will be forwarded to the author when you send them to *zauthor@zondervan.com*.

With Zondervan: Submit your review of this book by writing to *zreview@zondervan.com*.

Free Online Resources at
www.zondervan.com

Daily Bible Verses and Devotions: Enrich your life with daily Bible verses or devotions that help you start every morning focused on God. Visit www.zondervan.com/newsletters.

Free Email Publications: Sign up for newsletters on Christian living, academic resources, church ministry, fiction, children's resources, and more. Visit www.zondervan.com/newsletters.

Zondervan Bible Search: Find and compare Bible passages in a variety of translations at www.zondervanbiblesearch.com.

Other Benefits: Register to receive online benefits like coupons and special offers, or to participate in research.